# Bible-driven Youth Ministry

## Using the Bible to Support Working with Young People

**Tim Gough**
Pioneer Director, Youth for Christ in Wales

**GROVE BOOKS LIMITED**
**RIDLEY HALL RD CAMBRIDGE CB3 9HU**

# Contents




**Acknowledgments**

Huge thanks to the many students from different Bible colleges, particularly Cliff College, who have been through many iterations of the content of this booklet in lecture form. For all your patience, feedback and thirst for learning.





**First Impression** March 2022
**ISSN** 1748-3492
**ISBN** 978 1 78827 227 8

# Introduction

# 1

In the beginning God *spoke*—and stuff went everywhere!

That is the power of God's voice, right? When God speaks, creation happens. There is infinite creational power contained in the very words of God. The same is true today: when we hear from God, new things are made in us. And God is still speaking.

That same infinite creational power is contained in the Bible—where we find the very words of God. When we read it, God speaks and stuff is made in us. When we teach from it, stuff is made in those who hear. So why do we want to cling so tightly to the Bible in all we say and do? Because we want stuff-makingness to be happening all around us, all the time![1]

The Bible is such a gift. It is a cave full of treasure with a wide-open door. And we are handed shovels, buckets and JCB excavators and we are literally told to *help ourselves.* It is a table, ready-laid with an epic feast. A Masterchef banquet the likes of which even Gordon Ramsay could not imagine, and we are given a free seat at that table, a napkin, a couple of spoons and are told to *tuck in.*

Sounds good, right? The treasure, the feast, the infinite-creational power of God—which fits in our pocket, on our bedside table or on a mobile app. Every time we read it, we are the better for it. So, the question then becomes, *do we?*

Do we dig, loading up our buckets with treasure? Do we unfold our napkin, grab our two spoons and tuck in? Do we know it, love it, read it, treasure it, learn it, memorize it, examine it? Do we read it again and again like the well-thumbed copy of our favourite novel? Or the fading paper of an old love letter?

As youth workers and pastors, the slightly more awkward question becomes, *if we do not, then can we really be sure we are actually doing the right things?* Scary, huh?

## A Hungry, Hungry Hippo

When I was a kid, one of my favourite games was *Hungry, Hungry Hippos.* For those of you who were born more recently, this was a type of board game with a plastic tray, a whole bunch of tiny coloured balls and four spring loaded hippos. You would slam your palm down on your hippo's switch and it would then spring into the tray, mouth wide open, and take a huge bite, grabbing as many of the little balls as possible.

It is a pretty indecent way to eat, and a voracious game for four boisterous children to play!

I think that should be our approach to the Bible. We should not have a little nibble here and there; we should want to take huge bites! This does not necessarily mean we should try and read as much as we can as quickly as we can (although it could not hurt, right?); it means we should have an insatiable appetite for God's words.

In the book of Amos (big cheer for the first Bible quote in the booklet about Bible ministry in a chapter about reading the Bible), there was a serious famine going on. A famine is one of those horrible disasters countries face when they run out of something essential to their survival—usually food! Everyone begins to starve and they *crave* for just one small bite, one measly morsel—anything to sustain them.

But the famine in Amos was not a famine of food, or water, or shelter or safety. Amos 8.11 says:

> 'Behold, the days are coming,' declares the Lord GOD, 'when I will send a famine on the land—not a famine of bread, nor a thirst for water, but of hearing the words of the LORD.'

They needed, desperately, to hear from God. Not hearing from God was, to them, like starving. It says that their worship songs would turn to wails of pain (vv 8 and 10) and that their people would be lost and aimless (v 12). They were terrified! Being cut off from God's voice was like being cut off from life itself. They felt lost and vulnerable without it. They needed it and they did not have it. Not to break the mood, but they were hungry, hungry hippos, with no little coloured balls to eat!

If you are from Amos' time and you jump in the nearest Tardis and time-travel to visit us today, what do you expect to see? I imagine you expect to see the people of God *feasting* on the word at every chance they get. But *is* that what you would see?

A study by LifeWay Research in America found that 55% of regular church attenders did not actually read their Bibles more than once a week, and one in five simply never read it—ever.[2] The story is no better in the UK. A ComRes survey[3] found that only 35% of churchgoers read their Bibles every day, and a YouGov report found that only 14% of young people could properly differentiate a Bible story from other children's stories and fairy tales.[4]

This does not sound too good, right?

## The Effect on Our Resources

Consider that reading the Bible in a year is seen as quite a spiritual feat, but in reality, it only takes three 5-minute sittings a day. We spend four times that eating and drinking and nearly eight times that on social media.

What about knowing the whole biblical drama so thoroughly that we can place any story or character or idea into its larger context, understanding the links and history that support it, and applying it relevantly to the twenty-first century? This is surely a worthwhile venture, and a reasonable expectation for *any* Christian minister charged with teaching others.

I think the sad thing is that we see this lack of attentiveness to the Bible in our own resources. A few years back I was editing a Bible study for a well-known youth resource on the story of David and Goliath in 1 Samuel 17. The session, in many ways, was great! Well balanced, good fun, creative, participatory and with clear formational ideas. All the things good youth work teaching should be and exactly what you should expect from a high-quality resource! When it got to the passage however, everything fell apart.

The writer said, 'David defeated Goliath because David was *strong*, David was *skilled*, David was *able*, and David *knew who he was*!' There was no mention of God at all. I am all for teaching on the clarity of identity—but this story is not about David's skills, prowess or great strength. The story is pretty clearly about God; God's honour, God's glory and God's bonkers ability to use the rejected and the unexpected. This is definitely a 'just look at how epic God is' passage with a 'he can use anybody to accomplish amazing things' application. How many of our youth work resources miss the point in just this way? How many of our talks?

I think that one of the root causes of this famine can be found on our bookcases. Take a minute and go to a popular daily study guide—either on paper or online. I am guessing it will begin with a single verse or a very short story from the Bible. This might be followed by a much longer explanation, perhaps a reflective activity and, I imagine, an almost self-help focus on you, the individual. Many Bible studies and youth study resources follow this pattern of proof-text with explanation and reflection with a broad focus on making you feel good: very gently challenged, yet still comfortable. An ordinary Bible study guide can be read in five minutes and—with fuller reflection—is usually over in twenty at most.

**Has Bible study become an exercise in convenience?**

Has Bible study become an exercise in convenience? Designed to help us quickly fit it in with our busy lifestyle? This kind of interaction with the Bible requires very little from us as readers. The shovels, wheelbarrows and JCB excavators are left collecting cobwebs. We leave with trinkets but miss the gold. It is now possible that we have become so used to the trinkets that we just do not know what we are missing.

In Luke 24, Jesus appears on the road to Emmaus to two disciples. In v 27 Jesus explains how the whole Bible (well, as much as they had at the time!), all pointed back to himself. At the end of the walk in v 32, they say to each other, 'Didn't our hearts *burn* within us?' When? At the end of the God-slot with the moving video clip and well-timed piece of music in the perfect minor key? No. The disciples are clear that their hearts burned within them 'when [Jesus] opened the Scriptures to [them].'

To teach something relevantly in a way that genuinely equips a young person to connect with God, you have to know it deeply. To know something deeply, you have to spend time with it.

## The Effect on Our Ministry

I wonder if this generalized lack of confidence in, and competence with, the Bible has had a measurable impact on how we do youth ministry. If we were to pull on the threads of all that we do with young people today, would we find the Bible woven throughout—and if not, how much of a problem does that create?

The bold question to ask is: *is youth work itself fundamentally flawed without clear, specific and solid Bible-driven principles undergirding it?* It is a bold question and one that I think many of us would struggle to answer. But to be really honest, I wonder how many churches really demand this from their youth workers?

I think that there is a magic word, known throughout the Western church, for youth work—a word that magnificently summarizes the complex needs and rich desires that the church has towards its work with young people. That word is *something.*

> 'We need *something* for the teenagers.'
> 'Can we hire someone to do *something* with the kids?'

*Something,* however, does not demand a vibrant tapestry of theology, or really any biblical knowledge. *Something* does not require us to undergird our youth ministry with this foundation of well-thought-through, Bible-driven principles. *Something*—at its most monstrous—creates a youth work that develops independently from the church and independently from the Bible.

A sign of this is a youth ministry that changes shape every six months or so as one idea is exhausted and another is needed to stoke the fires of novelty.

Novelty, unfortunately, is fickle and short-lived. It is a bit like a stone skipping on a pond: it will bounce for a while and maybe travel quite a way, but eventually it will stop and sink.

I want to contend that this relentless drive for *something* has made us a little woolly around the edges. We need to be honest and truly look at the implications of proof-texted daily readings, spoon-fed Bible stories and broadly low expectations for God's work in youth ministry. If today's youth workers were *yesterday's* youth, then we have our work cut out for us nurturing young people who can build *tomorrow's* church.

*Something* just is not enough.

# 2

# The Lingering Curse of the One-eared Mickey Mouse

When I started writing, this chapter came last. I have moved it to the beginning for a simple reason—if youth ministry is a biblical concept, then it should probably sit under or within a theology of church. It is really hard to attempt a biblical look at working with young people if we do not start by seeing the entire body of Jesus, the church, as a significant part of that work.

So, although there are specific ways to work with young people in the Bible, which we will get to, if we do not begin by looking at the whole puzzle together, and in one piece, the bits later will make no sense. So, we begin here—with a poor injured Mickey.

In the 1980s, one quick-witted youth worker described the relationship between the *church* and the *youth ministry* as 'the one-eared Mickey Mouse.'[5] The diagram below shows you why it is called that! The idea is that the church and the youth group had become two separate entities, connected…*ish*, even linked…*kinda*—but not truly one thing. Although his idea was initially dismissed out of hand, in the years that followed, more authors started to push back against the homogenous youth group. We now have so many books and articles pushing back against the curse of the one-eared Mickey Mouse that it feels like we really should have shifted it by now. But, alas, it lives on!

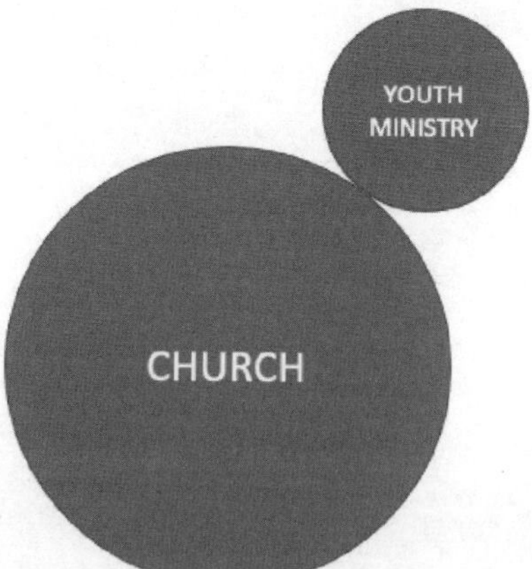

The Bible is clear that church is one body, not a dismembered collection of limbs. Specialist approaches to teaching and worship will always be important, but for youth ministry (and for that matter children's, women's, family, third-age, men's, etc ministries) to thrive, it needs to fundamentally begin from a place of holistic togetherness.

A few years ago, when I was sitting my MA, a group of full-time children's workers from a big city church came in to speak to us. They all looked far more cool than was entirely decent (you do not *all* need to shop at All Saints!), and they really believed that they had cracked children's ministry. They told us, with buoyant excitement, how their Sunday mornings worked. It went something like this:

> Ok, so each family rocks up in their car, they get out and they each go to their separate buildings. The parents go to their building, the youth go to theirs and the children have their own special building too. It's brilliant! Everyone's needs are met, and the parents get time off too. At the end of the Sunday morning, they all meet back up again at the car.

They were so excited about their Sunday morning strategy, but it made me want to scream.

## A Whole Body is a Happy Body!

Let me ask a pedantic question: *if I was to saw off your legs and place them in a box twelve feet away from the rest of you, are you or your legs going to be particularly happy about it? What about in ten years' time—will it get better? What if you were to duct tape them back on?* Bodies are designed beautifully and perfectly to work as one holistic unit.

Staying with the somewhat gruesome theme, a severed hand—less comically like Thing from the *Adams Family* and more like a scene from *Saw*—cut from the body and left on the table will actually move. It will twitch for a while and will exhibit what looks like active signs of life. In fact, a severed hand can survive for up to twelve hours in a warm environment, and up to several days if properly refrigerated. Now there is something nice to tell your children!

Let us be honest though, this hand is not really alive. A twitch is not voluntary or intentional movement. For all intents and purposes, when it is removed from the body it becomes a dead limb.

My late uncle Bob was awesome. I always thought he was a real-life pirate; he even had a hook for a hand! In reality, he served in the British Navy and lost his arm in an explosion during the Falklands War. His arm was damaged in the blast beyond repair, so he had to have it amputated. When I was a child, I asked him innocently, 'Hey, so what did you do with your severed arm—did you keep it in a big glass jar?' To which he simply replied, 'Binned it. Didn't work anymore.' My uncle Bob knew it, and so do we. It is pretty basic physiology after all—our bodies do *much* better when they are in one piece!

This goes for any and every limb that we hack off the body and put into its own contained and homogenous ecosystem. Glass jars just do not work. The question this raises is just how many limbs can be removed from the body, and for how long, before the body itself becomes just another one of these dead limbs? The more we chop the church up into smaller and more specific groups, the more the whole body suffers.

**The more we chop the church up into smaller groups, the more the whole body suffers**

Whether knowingly or not, we strategically use a cellular model—where if you divide a cell, it produces more cells. So, the thought is that if we divide up the church into smaller, homogenous, missionally-contained groups, then we will see numerical growth. This approach, however, just does not jive with *any* of the relationship metaphors in the Bible. Instead, the Bible focuses on family, marriage, organisms etc; things that suffer when you break them up.

If our focus is on cutting limbs off the body, rather than seeing each limb as part of a larger coherent unit, then how we treat each limb will be, by nature, slightly weird. How we seek to meet its needs, attempt to make it healthy and try to help it grow will always look slightly strange when compared to any efforts made for a limb that is actually attached to a body. At best, these separated limbs become resource heavy. *Crazy* resource heavy, and ultimately always unsustainable. Whether this is after months or even decades, the damage always eventually shows.

A youth group that is essentially separate from the life of the church is effectively a limb in a glass jar. This contained ecosystem can never be as healthy as it *could be* if connected into the body it came from.

When limbs are separate from the body, it does not really matter how healthy looking or *large* they are in the short term. They have a half-life. Spending efforts bulking up a limb that is separate from the body is a very sad exercise, and one which will not bear long-term fruit. Even a large youth group that is essentially disconnected from the people of God will always be denying something foundational to both the young people and the church. Give this a few decades or more and you start to see the overall health of both groups evaporate across the entire church. So, have we done this? Have we institutionalized an amputation? Have we inadvertently organized a split, or a schism, right down the middle of the church?

## Reimagining Young People and the Church

This is a booklet about youth work, but in reality, it is about the church. Youth worker, if you have been given this book by your pastor, you might want to check that they have read it first and if not, give it back!

However well it has been done in isolation, youth work represents a lot of what has gone wrong with the modern church, simply because it is the most common limb that gets lopped off the church. However, as a lifelong committed youth worker, I also believe that youth work is where the restoration of church needs to begin.

**Youth work is where the restoration of church needs to begin**

If our subversive, and yet relentless, pursuit is for *a bigger youth group*, and we are trying to achieve that in a separate eco-system away from the wider church, then we have probably bought into the big youth group myth.

The *big youth group myth* subversively underlies so many of our strategies, resources and practices. It lies hidden inside our vision statements, job adverts and annual reports. The *big youth group myth* says that if the church has a big youth group, then those young people, and the church they are connected to, will both be healthy. I believe this is a myth because in seventy-five years of trying it has not produced the results we all hoped for.

Let us begin by re-examining this myth that has sat so proudly at the heart of decades of church-based youth ministry. Perhaps if we do, we can begin to make changes that will lead to a living, flourishing body of Christ.

For youth ministry to be truly biblical, it needs to play a much bigger role in the unity of the church. As tempting as it is, we cannot continue just to keep doing our own thing. This is about more than making church youth friendly, adding a drum kit, shortening the sermons or serving Red Bull after the service (do not do that!). We need a fundamental perception shift about what church really is, and how young people are a part of that. The reality is that without church there is no healthy youth ministry, and without young people, church will also be a far weaker and ultimately ill-fated body.

Armed with this wide-angle lens on young people and the church, we will move on now to examine exactly who young people were in the Bible and what God's desire for their adolescent development was *within* God's people.

# 3 So, is Youth Ministry Actually in the Bible?

Why yes, yes, it is. Kinda…ish. But no, not really. I mean you are not going to find lock-ins and nerf wars in the Bible. Sorry! That does not mean do not do them though…although if you are still doing lock-ins, then you are a braver youth worker than I! What we need to examine is the heartbeat, or the basic essence of youth work in the Bible.

We need to discover if the Bible treats young people—particularly adolescents—as a distinct and particular group. If we decide they are one, then we need to explore what God designed this time of youth to be for—in a broad-brush way. For what purpose did God design young people *as* young people? And once we have done that, we need to look at some of the more specific ways the Bible lays out for working with young people. So, let us start where everyone wants to start a chapter like this—with a hard exploration of dense Hebrew syntax. Whoop!

## Young People are a Distinct Group in the Bible

I think that, compared to the Bible, we break our groups up *way* too much. God's people always did stuff together. When Israel crossed the Red Sea, they did not go across in their separate groups. There was not a *senior's Scrabble group*, or *a men's bacon-breakfast posse* (for more than one reason), or a *Sunday school section* complete with juice boxes and name tags. The adults did not go through the Exodus alone, nor were the children excluded when Moses read out the Ten Commandments. Young people were always there.

That all said, it is also important to understand that young people and children were still seen as distinct groups *within* Israel. We need to be clear that they were not separate groups filtered *out*, but distinct groups *within*. So, they mostly did stuff together, but were helped to grow and develop within their specific age ranges too.

One of the clearest ways we can see this is by looking at how different age ranges are consistently referred to using different words throughout the Bible.

Children have their own Hebrew words in the Old Testament. *Yeled,* for instance, refers to boys under the age of 12. Then there are fun words like *taph, gamul, 'awil,* which are all used to talk about infants, babies or dependants. Then there is the cracking word *yoneq,* which is an organic word that usually appears with developing children in passages that say something like 'He grew up like a young shoot.' Love that! But *none* of these are about young people.

So, there are distinct words for children and there are words for adults too. Between these, however, there is another specific lexical category: *young people.* Ecclesiastes 11.9 is a great illustration of this:

> Be happy, *young man,* while you are *young* and let your heart give you joy in the days of your *youth.*

So, in this super short verse, three of the four main Hebrew words for youth all appear together. Let us take a look at them: [6]

> '...*young man': bachuwr* means a youth of fighting age—so old enough to join the army (Isa 31.8), but unmarried without dependent children to look after (Ruth 3.10).
>
> '...while you are *young': yalduwth* is a contained timeframe for being young. It is a way of saying childhood, boyhood, girlhood or even just youth (Ps 110.3).
>
> And '...days of your *youth': bĕchurowth* is something like a collective noun for a group of young people, or another timeframe of youth (Num 11.28).

So, these guys and girls are of fighting age (mostly guys) and around the age for marriage (13–18 depending on sex—the girls tended to marry younger). They were also too young to pay temple tax, making them under the age of 20 (Exod 30.11–16). We are talking roughly 12–19-year-olds—teenagers!

Young people *did* exist in the Bible then. They were a distinct people group *within* the body of God's people in the Old Testament, but not separate from it.

## Young People are Made with a Distinct Purpose

I recently ran a consultation night with a bunch of young people on how they wanted a youth centre to look. At one point a girl asked me, 'Hey, do you want to know how to make gingerbread?' 'Sure,' I replied. To which she responded, 'You just hold a slice of bread up over your face!' She yelled loudly, giggling wildly, and waving her arms in the air.

For context: I have ginger hair.

Then she and three other girls spent a good chunk of time writing the word 'bread' on as many post-it notes as they could find and stuck them to everything (and everyone) in the room. It was, frankly, really odd.

I remember stopping for a moment and thinking to myself, *why?* Why are you teenagers so…teenager-y? I mean, what is the point? Have you ever done that? Just stopped mid-youth-group and just looked at the teenage condition and wondered to yourself: *why? Why do you even exist!*

So, let us have a look. Knowing that young people in the Bible were seen as a distinct group, why did they exist? Why did God make the adolescent? Did he mean to? Or did he just sneeze when drawing the line between 'child' and adult? Why does this period of youth exist?

Starting with Prov 1.10–19, and Prov 5.1–6, we discover that the time of youth is the pivotal and ideal time for a person to develop *wisdom*. This may seem obvious, but sometimes we confuse *wisdom* with *knowledge*, and think that because we have one, we necessarily have the other. You can have all the knowledge in the world—like all the pieces of a car laid out in the sun—but without the wisdom to put them together and drive, you have got nothing but a heap of rusting metal and rubber.

The wisdom in Proverbs—and specifically for young people in those two passages—is more than the wisdom that leaves the tomato out of a fruit salad. It is a life-defining wisdom that helps young people clearly see and identify sin and poor choices, and it is the wisdom that guides them actively to reject temptation. This wisdom helps them to recognize the best path when several are presented, and it teaches them to make increasingly healthy choices over how they live. Considering that adolescence is a melting pot of tumultuous hormones, social cartwheeling and life-defining choices, it makes sense that the authors of Proverbs see this time as the best catalyst to learn this heart-skill. Throughout Proverbs we see that wisdom is best developed within a worshipping community of believers.

**Wisdom is best developed within a worshipping community of believers**

Moving to the New Testament passages, 1 Tim 5.1–8 explains the immensely graceful and real-world ways in which young people are called to interact with those who are older and in need, and vv 11–15 expands this through the values of developing a family. 1 Peter 5.5–7 helpfully summarizes these aspects as mutual submission, humility and respect. Put another way, youth is a time to learn to become a functional part of the wider community.

The Old Testament passages I chose focus on the *inward journey* of adolescence—developing a wisdom-filled relationship with God, with plenty of help from the worshipping community. The New Testament passages looked at the *outward journey* of becoming a healthy and functional part of the community of faith.

So young people need the whole church body as they learn how to relate to God and each other. To be observers of—and real participants in—its worship and to be integral parts of its relational activity. Again, there truly is no youth ministry without church, and church is far worse off without young people.

## The 'Youth Work of the Bible' Vision Statement

I love a good vision—or mission, or purpose—statement! We have probably all got one. Anyone who has read Doug Field's *Purpose Driven Youth Ministry* from the late 1990s, probably has theirs filled with trigger verbs and actionable clauses—on big cheesy posters![7] The question we have to ask ourselves, though, is whether our vision statement is in line with the Bible's vision, or purpose, for the time of youth.

I think, basically put, the Bible's vision or mission or purpose statement for youth ministry might be best summarized something like this:

> Youth is a distinct time to learn how to become a whole and healthy member of the worshipping community of faith.

Now, I know that is not sexy—it sounds quite ordinary actually. But it is true. This statement requires us to:

- Introduce young people to Jesus.
- Integrate them fully into a worshipping community of faith.
- Work with them on a continual journey from childhood to adulthood.
- Actively encourage their participation in all levels of church life and ministry.
- Give them the tools, mentoring and support they need to live holy lives and make good choices.

The question then becomes: do *our* youth ministry statements actively encourage these things? For want of a better way of putting it—do our visions for youth line up with the Bible's? I was curious about this so did a little bit of independent research and spent a few years collecting youth ministry vision, mission and purpose statements from around the world. There is a huge amount of overlap and similarities, with various levels of wit—and with, I think, some common and serious omissions. Here are a few typical ones that represent these common themes:

'To create *community* where youth *encounter* Jesus Christ and *respond* with their lives.'

'To provide a safe place for high-school students to learn about and practise the way of Jesus, together.'

'To help teenagers discover life change through Jesus Christ.'

'To create an environment for young people to meet Jesus, make friends and get equipped.'

'To passionately help teens find and live out their identity in Jesus Christ.'

There is a lot to love and genuinely appreciate in these statements. There is a clear focus on the particulars of working with teenagers. There is a drive for them to know Jesus. There is a passion for the gospel. There is also a push towards ongoing life change. This is all great—and we would not want to lose any of this!

However, none of these statements clearly connect young people to the broader worshipping body of faith—the church—in such a way that that connection itself helps them grow in wisdom. Do not get me wrong! I really appreciate the missional focus and the love, but there is something very one-eared Mickey Mouse about these statements.

If we want our young people truly to thrive, and for our youth ministry practices to be sewn into the rich tapestry of the Bible, then we need to pro-actively and intentionally connect young people more to the wider church as a fundamental part of their development. Sure, church needs to adapt for this to work too, but we are limiting a young person's growth, longevity and stability by trying to keep them in our own little contained youth-work ecosystems. Youth workers are not the whole package, after all.[8]

God's purpose for youth involves far, far more than just youth work, and youth workers alone cannot provide it.

# 4

# The First Ever Youth Workers

Young people are essential to the biblical narrative. I am not using hyperbole; if we were to take the teenaged characters out of the Bible, the overarching story would simply collapse. Many crucial events in God's word find a young person centre stage. Just ponder for a moment what some of the Bible's heroes accomplished, *when they were young people.*[9]

- *Rebekah*—Showed incredible faith by serving and consenting to marry Isaac, journeying with him into the unknown (Genesis 24).
- *Joseph*—Rejects sexual sin when advanced upon by a powerful, older woman (Genesis 39).
- *Samuel*—Called to speak to God's nation during their most fearful and difficult times (1 Samuel 3).
- *David*—Defends God's honour and holiness against a giant (1 Samuel 17).
- *Esther*—Risks taking a plot against her people to the king, saving many (Esther 2).
- *Josiah*—Lives righteously before the Lord as a child, and diligently pursues God as a teenage king (2 Kings 22).
- *Daniel*—Commits to remaining pure in Babylon surrounded by idolatry that makes our world look tame (Daniel 1).
- *Mary*—Remained a virgin and trusted in God's promise of a virgin birth (Luke 1).
- *Jesus* (worth mentioning, right!)—Even taught his elders, and grew in wisdom, in stature and in favour with God and men (Luke 2).

At the very heart of God there is the heart of a youth worker. He simply loves to use young people and does uncommonly world-changing things with them as a matter of course. Having *this* perspective lifts our expectations—and even starts to shape how we approach our youth work projects and strategy. Young people are the church *right now*, after all.

## Why Young People?

In the Rio 2016 Olympics, Andy Murray defended his title and won another tennis gold medal. Amazing, but not especially surprising considering his packed medal cabinet. I, however, am *terrible* at tennis! I took lessons a few years back in London but dropped out quickly when it was clear that I was just a danger to myself and others. When I pick up a racquet, people run and hide.

If you turned on your television and saw *me* winning the gold medal at Rio, you would be looking for the trick. You would think it was a spoof, or that something fishy was going on. You would look *beyond* me for a coach, medical team, or even a miracle drug!

Similarly, when young people do incredible things, people tend to look beyond them for something more. This makes us look for God. When God uses the ordinary, the unexpected and the rejected we are left in no doubt that *he* did it. We are drawn into the sure knowledge that he is mighty. Young people become a portal that opens out into a heavenly viewpoint, bringing a vibrant perspective to bear on our God that might have otherwise gone unseen.

The Bible is full, then, of the stories of young people connecting with God and his people. However, in many of these stories we also find a committed, connected, and concerned adult guiding and leading them. They had youth workers.

We can learn so much for our practice from these biblical examples of something akin to youth workers. I am going to give a snapshot here from just a couple of example stories with some applications, but if you would like more of this—I wrote a whole book about it called *Rebooted: Reclaiming Youth Ministry for the Long Haul—A Biblical Framework.*

## Eli

Samuel's relationship to his youth worker Eli began before he was even born, when Eli prayed with Samuel's mother Hannah (1 Sam 1.10–20). Eli was there from the very beginning, offering Samuel to the Lord alongside Hannah (1 Sam 1.24–28). This is a great image of a leader teaming up with parents. Samuel moved into the tabernacle and began his education.

Eli continued to live with, teach, train and mentor young Samuel until he was very old, even though Samuel 'did not yet know the Lord' (1 Sam 3.7). He drew him into worship just as Abraham did with Isaac, he taught him what God was like and he taught him to recognize God's voice.

During the call of Samuel, although it took a few tries, Eli recognized God was speaking to Samuel, named it and taught him how to listen and respond (1 Sam 3.8–9). From there Samuel began his incredible journey with God.

### Where Is God Already Working?

One of the first principles we can pull out from this passage is seeing where God is already at work, naming it and then developing it. Eli recognizes God speaking to Samuel, points it out and instructs Samuel how to respond to it. Is there any better role for a youth worker?

We do not create God in young people, we do not lead God to people and we do not make faith happen. We look for where God is *already* at work in their lives and we name it.

The most significant thing we can do for a young person is to teach them to hear God's voice, listen to his instruction and then respond wholeheartedly in worship and obedience. Our job is to recognize God's voice in their lives when they cannot, teach them to recognize it and then respond to it:

> 'Here I am.'

## Samuel and Saul

This legacy continues as Samuel chooses King David. In 1 Samuel 16 'ruddy David,' the runt of the litter, was chosen by God to be king. God did not consider his outward appearance (as *we* might). God kept to his habit of doing the extraordinary with the ordinary and the unbelievable with the unexpected.

During this time, in 1 Samuel 17, David famously defeats the ridiculous, undefeated Philistine champion Goliath. Young (1 Sam 17.33) David's tangible zeal for holiness (1 Sam 17.26) and unwavering faith in God's protection (1 Sam 17. 37) banishes the enemy army. King Saul (now there is an unexpected youth worker!) does not dampen David's enthusiasm or douse his faith. Instead, he does all he can to equip David—and then he lets him loose, the fate of the Israelites on his shoulders: 'Go, and the LORD be with you' (1 Sam 17.37).

### Let Them Try Their Strength

It is all too easy to numb or undermine a young person's zeal when we judge it by the light of our adult experience. A quality youth worker, however, will recognize the signs of a living and developing relationship with God and will let their young people try their strengths. Young people have incredible capacity for faith and have far less in the way of filters and baggage than we perhaps might.

The nature of grace demands that we let young people make mistakes, which contrasts strongly with our culture's desire to bubble wrap and safeguard children from any and all potential harm, or even to safeguard ourselves from the potential upset and mayhem they are sure to bring down upon us. If Samuel had not been responsive to the voice of God when picking David, and if Saul had not given his trust to the shepherd boy delivering the packed lunch—then the Bible, and indeed history, would have gone very differently.

## Paul

In Acts 20.9 we meet young Eutychus, falling asleep in a window box, three storeys up.

He was not being watched, but was left droopy, ignored and unnoticed—until he fell to his death (Acts 20.9). Only Paul saw. This is bonkers—in a room of adults, why did no-one say, 'Hey buddy, just come down from that ledge, there's a good lad.' Only Paul sees—and what does Paul do?

Paul went down to Eutychus. Down from his speaker's platform, down from his position of authority, down through storey one, down through storey two, down through storey three, down to the street, down to the ground, down *flat*, and threw himself on this young person. It is almost an image of sharing in his death.

Paul came out *from*—and in *to*: Out *from* his place of security, comfort, authority, respect and safety, and in *to* the very darkest, most exposed place of brokenness and tragedy. He then lies across the broken, bloodied body of this young boy on the pavement, wraps his arms around him and embraces him. It is hard not to see the deep, moving well of compassion in that action.

Paul went down to where there was death, and he covered Eutychus in compassion—literally lay across him, and then, of course, Jesus through that act of love brought Eutychus back to life (Acts 20.10).

### Openly Cover in Compassion

Surely the principle here is simple. Notice young people, see their needs, come out of your place of comfort and into the world they inhabit. Come to their level and openly cover them in compassion. See them, go to them, love them.

Now hopefully you will have policies in place that prevent you from *actually lying on top of a young person*—do not do that! Luckily there are an infinite number of other ways to show them the love and compassion of our God without hurting anyone or losing your job.

## Parents

We should not consider youth workers in the Bible without spending time with parents. Parents are—ideally—the best suited for youth work.

In Deut 6.1–7 we learn that it was primarily the parent's responsibility (with the support of the whole people of God, see Deut 5.1) to share their faith with their children and bring them up as believers.

The teachings of God would be written on anything that stayed still long enough (like door frames, Deut 6.9) and tied to things that did not stay still (like hands and foreheads, Deut 6.8). They would be talked about and sung about at every meal and on every journey. If Israel were obedient to this Deuteronomy passage, then a young person could not swing a ferret without coming across something that told them something about God.

Young people should grow with the promises and commands of God as a daily part of their reality at home in the family. The job of youth workers, in part, is to do all we can to support, equip and train parents and carers in this mammoth task.

Deuteronomy 6.7 tells us that young people need to be *impressed* with these things. The word 'impress' is emphatic. It conjures images of a potter pushing a finger into wet clay before it hardens, moulding the shape while it is still pliable. God's truths should leave a healthy, solid and lasting impression. Young people, moving through the developmental stages of growth, should mature into a relationship with God organically within their family. This means that it should be a solid part of their reality during their formation.

### Supporting the Family

Youth work begins and ends in the home with the *parents*. They are given the privilege of being the primary movers in the faith development of a young person.[10] Throughout the Old Testament we see constant reminders of just how intimately involved parents should be with the faith development of their children. Of course, this does not always work, and as youth leaders we know just how difficult parents can be!

**Youth work begins and ends in the home with the parents**

I was once told by a dad that he had stopped reading the Bible with his son because that was now 'my job.' A mum once told me that I was a 'dangerous sexist' because I 'wouldn't let her daughter sing in the worship team.' (The real reason she did not sing was because she did not *want* to sing in the worship team, but also did not want to tell mum!) An American youth leader I know was once asked by a parent, 'Are you going to teach my child what sex is?' to which he responded, 'No, that's your job. I'll teach about sexual morality, but the mechanics are up to you.' He never saw that family again. We all know that parents can be whole heaps of fun.

There is more to this though. Over 42% of marriages in the UK (and 40–50% in the USA) end in divorce, and almost half of those affect children under the age of 16.[11] Further, the rapid decline of Christianity means fewer believing parents.[12] Relying *exclusively* on parents to develop the faith journeys of their children just is not realistic.

This is why young people and parents are supposed to be supported by the whole believing body of God's people. This would be the *church* today. Youth work is the work of the *whole church*. Every member of God's people bears a responsibility to display, model and to some degree, teach the truths of God. This supports the parents in a wide network of accountability, and can be facilitated by a quality youth worker.

# 5

# The First Ever Youth Group

## Was Jesus a Youth Worker?

Although this title may produce a frowny face at first glance, it is not quite as pedantic a question as you might think.

What we call youth ministry today is in reality only about 50–70 years old. So, in that sense, no, Jesus was not a youth worker. He did not run nerf battles, ice-cream parties, or—heaven forbid—lock ins! However, at a far more fundamental level, Jesus conducted the vast majority of his ministry with something akin to a youth group. Let us poke at *that* idea.

## How Old Were the Disciples?

How old do you think the disciples were when Jesus chose them? If you look at Renaissance art, modern movies, or even children's Bibles, you might think they were middle-aged or even older men. They all seem to have long white beards and shiny heads!

I believe, however, that there is enough said in the Bible to conclude the disciples were comprised of young people when they were chosen—mostly teenagers and maybe a couple of young twenty-somethings. We are going to dust off some of the evidence here so you can make up your own mind!

First, we learn in Luke 3.23 that Jesus was a young rabbi at only age 30 and, in that tradition, would not have chosen followers older than himself (in fact, at 30, any potential students might have been choosing their own followers). It was pretty common for a rabbi to be followed around by a small group of teenagers. This might explain why Peter is the only disciple that we are told was married, suggesting that the other disciples, including his little brother Andrew, were just not old enough (Matt 8.14).

Sticking with the rabbi stuff, most of Jesus' disciples were Jewish, so had been through the first stages of Jewish education, *Bet Sefer* (ages 5–13). Between 13–16, however, only a small number of *very* successful (or crazy-wealthy!) students would have been chosen to follow a rabbi, which they then did until they turned 30. If they were not chosen, they would have been apprenticed in a trade, usually by their father, for a few years before taking off on their own. This is when Jesus chooses fishermen James, John and Andrew: during apprenticeship with their dad. They did not make the grade; they had been bypassed—until they met Jesus. Jesus called these guys *teknion,* which is an affectionate term meaning little kids, which might have been more than a little insulting if they were all grown men (John 13.33)!

Next, temple taxes were only paid by those over the age of twenty (Exod 30.13–14), so Jesus instructs Peter in Matt 17.27 to do so—but only for himself and Peter. The other disciples are right there, but Jesus does not ask any of these other disciples to pay *their* tax (Matt 17.22–24). I think that is because they were not yet old enough.

Finally, we need to put our biology heads on! Lifespans were shorter then than they are today, and many of the disciples had long and fruitful ministries after Pentecost. For instance, John wrote Revelation at least sixty years after Jesus rose, so how old could he really have been when he was chosen? Were they all pushing 100 when they died?

**The disciples seem to have been a young group**

Peter *may* have been mid-twenties, and Matthew as a tax collector *could* have been a little older too (unless he was also an apprentice, which makes sense). So, all things considered, the disciples seem to have been a young group. I know, in the conventional or contemporary sense that they are not *really* a youth group with a fancy name and cool hoodies, but that does not change them being a group of young people.

## What Did this First Youth Group Do?

Jesus never called anybody to be pew-fodder. He begins by giving his disciples a clear life-defining purpose, '*Follow me and I will show you how to fish for people*' (Matt 4.19). The disciples have a mission, a purpose and a job to do—right from the start, not when they get saved. There is no bait-and-switch, and no massive evangelism event. Jesus starts with the few who show up, and he gets on with it.

Jesus then spent three whole years just pouring into them. He lived with them, ate with them, travelled with them, told stories to them, sang songs with them, prayed with them and taught them.

At first, the disciples just *observe* what Jesus does and try to make sense of it chatting with him. Then Jesus starts to give them *little jobs* to do ('tell them to sit down,' 'feed them'), involving them, correcting and giving confidence to them. Eventually Jesus *sends them out* to try their strengths, and they begin doing it on their own, after which they return and debrief.

Pulling all that together, here is what you could very cheekily call the *Jesus model of youth ministry*:

- Start with the few who turn up
- Give young people a life-defining purpose from the off
- Share (with healthy boundaries) your life with them
- Teach them clearly and constantly
- Start to get them involved in your ministry
- Send them out to do it themselves
- Debrief and repeat

What is striking here is that it is entirely unclear when Jesus stopped evangelizing his disciples and started discipling them. This could make our usual lines in the sand (and our subsequent programme strategies) a little presumptuous and exclusionary.

## So, Was Jesus a Youth Worker?

Like us? No, but should we be youth workers *like him?* Yes, yes and a thousand times, yes! By focusing on smaller groups, giving them meaning and purpose and getting them involved early, we could be setting young people up for a great life of faith!

It is interesting to consider *how* Jesus taught his disciples. We know that he spent time with the twelve, but we also know that he gave extra, specific times to three: Peter, James and John (Mark 9.2; Matt 26.37).

It is possible, when looking at the numbers, that each of these three also went on to spend time with three other disciples. 3+(3x3)=12, so every disciple was discipled one-to-one. This is a little speculative, but it might explain why the disciples are first listed in six pairs (Matthew 10) and sent out two by two (Mark 6.7). These multiples of 3 also work with the 72 sent out by Jesus later—suggesting that Jesus' followers grew exponentially through discipleship and were self-supporting through a mutual discipleship network. Neat, eh? At very least I think we can conclude that they were set up in a way that encouraged them to look after each other.

So, what about you? Think about this: If you saw 50 young people saved through your youth ministry each year for 50 years, you would see a total of 2,500 new disciples. That is amazing—and what a great legacy!

Consider, however, that if you discipled three young people every two years and taught them to do the same over 50 years, then two things would happen: *First*, you would probably lose your job for having a tiny, rubbish youth club. *Secondly*, you would see the entire world saved in just under half your lifetime. Take the day off!

Perhaps the right thing for us to do is step off the stage, commit ourselves to the few and teach them to do the same. Is not that what Jesus would do, after all?

# 6

# Conclusion

Whoop! Well done for making it to the end. If this was a YouTube video, then I would be telling you a secret word right about now to put into the comments, so I would know you had watched to the end.

Well, there is no secret word! Sorry. But I hope I have done enough to replace the *magic* word 'something' with a few key ideas.

*First,* church is fundamental to healthy youth ministry. You cannot truly have youth ministry without it, and church is far worse off without young people. Does this mean church needs to change? Sure! But so do we. There is work to be done on both sides of the one-eared Mickey Mouse but the perception that we are all emphatically one body is a good start.

*Secondly,* young people are a distinct group in the Bible, who do need specialist teaching. God's plan for youth was to help them learn how to become a whole and healthy member of the worshipping community of faith.

*Thirdly,* we need to help young people take responsibility over their own faith—like Eli did with Samuel; give them room to try their strengths and make mistakes—like Saul did with David; cover them in life-giving compassion alongside our teaching—like Paul did with Eutychus; and support, equip and champion parents and carers together as God's people—like Israel did in Deuteronomy 6.

*Fourthly,* just like Jesus we should focus on the few who show up, give them a life-defining purpose, teach them, send them off to share their faith, then debrief and repeat.

So, youth workers, let us start with church, supplement that with specialized ministry, help young people take responsibility and get involved, champion parents and then get out of the way! I think there is some good Bible-drivenness in there.

If you are interested in going deeper on this topic, this booklet is a mixture of some lecture notes and a summary of a larger book I wrote a few years ago for IVP called *Rebooted: Reclaiming Youth Ministry for the Long Haul—A Biblical Framework.* A lot of the material in here is expanded on there, with a lot more depth and practical suggestions. Maybe worth a read?

If in doubt, though, always go back to your Bible! When we read it, God speaks and stuff is made in us. When we teach from it, stuff is made in those who hear.

# Notes

1 This booklet contains an abridged version of some of the material in my larger book, T Gough, *Rebooted: Reclaiming Youth Ministry for the Long Haul—A Biblical Framework* (London: Inter-Varsity Press, 2018).

2 LifeWay Research: *Americans Are Fond of the Bible, Don't Actually Read It.* Available at: http://lifewayresearch.com/2017/04/25/lifeway-research-americans-are-fond-of-the-bible-dont-actually-read-it/

3 ComRes Research commissioned by The Bible Society: *Taking the Pulse.* Available at: http://www.biblesociety.org.uk/uploads/files/our_work/taking_the_pulse.pdf

4 YouGov Report commissioned by the Bible Society. Available at: *Pass it On*: http://www.biblesociety.org.uk/uploads/content/projects/Bible-Society-Report_030214_final_.pdf

5 Stuart Cummings-Bond, 'The One-Eared Mickey Mouse,' *Youth Worker Journal 6* (Fall 1989): 76–78.

6 For more discussion on the words in this verse see D Keehn, 'Biblical Mandate for Youth Ministry (Part 2): Youth Ministry in the Old Testament' (2012). Available at: https://www.biola.edu/blogs/good-book-blog/2012/biblical-mandate-for-youth-ministry-part-2-youth-ministry-in-the-old-testament

7 D Fields, *Purpose Driven Youth Ministry: 9 Essential Foundations for Healthy Growth* (Grand Rapids, MI: Zondervan, 1998).

8 For a great look at this question see A du Feu, *Looking Good Naked: Youth Work and the Body of Christ* (Oregon: Resource Publications, 2019).

9 K Turner, *Expanding the Expectations of Parents and Youth Workers.* Available at: http://ethomasmedia.com/cdg/audio/2009%20Seminars/expanding_the_expectations_of_parents_and_youth_workers_ke.mp3

10 For some of the best books working with Christian parents see R Turner, *Parenting Children for a Life of Confidence: Releasing Children to Live in God's Strength* (Abingdon: Bible Reading Fellowship, 2015) and R Turner, *Parenting Children for a Life of Purpose: Empowering Children to Become who they are Called to Be* (Abingdon: Bible Reading Fellowship, 2014).

11 Office for National Statistics (ONS) 2012–13. Various reports here. Available at: https://www.ons.gov.uk/peoplepopulationandcommunity/birthsdeathsandmarriages/divorce

12 2011 Census data via ONS. Available at: https://www.ons.gov.uk/census/2011census. For a broader discussion on this see both C Brown, *The Death of Christian Britain* (London: Routledge, 2001) and S Bruce, *God is Dead: Secularization in the West* (Religion in the Modern World) (Malden, MA: Blackwell, 2002).